Sunflowers

Sunflowers

MetroBooks

MetroBooks

An Imprint of Friedman/Fairfax Publishers

©2000 by Friedman/Fairfax Publishers

Library of Congress Cataloging-in-Publication Data available upon request.

ISBN 1-58663-066-0

Editor: Susan Lauzau
Designer: Andrea Karman
Photography Editor: Christopher C. Bain
Production Manager: Jeanne Hutter

Color separations by Ocean Graphics International Company Ltd.
Printed in China byLeefung-Asco Printers Ltd.

1 3 5 7 9 10 8 6 4 2

For bulk purchases and special sales, please contact:
Friedman/Fairfax Publishers
Attention: Sales Department
15 West 26th Street
New York, NY 10010
212/685-6610 FAX 212/685-1307

Visit our website:
www.metrobooks.com

...We are the Flower—Thou the Sun!

Forgive us, if as days decline—

We nearer steal to Thee!...

Emily Dickinson

Sunflowers

The sunflower presents an honest face to the world. Not a dainty plant, it refuses to mince its way through carefully choreographed flower borders. With a forthright presence it stands solid and tall, whether alone or in the cheerful company of its brethren. The sunflower is a friendly flower, in its natural state beaming with a welcoming aureole of golden petals. It is also an accommodating one, bearing a practical disk plentifully stuffed with seed for bird and beast. Very often sunflowers grow to the height of a small person, so they don't ask one to creep about on the ground, nor even stoop, to admire them closely. Sunflowers reward those who sow them with satisfyingly rapid and dramatic growth. Has the sunflower a dark side at all? How unlikely that seems.

For all the efforts of persistent plant breeders, the sunflower resists seeming entirely tamed, like a small well-scrubbed boy dressed in his "good" short pants that show dirty knees, with a cowlick no amount of brushing can subdue. Still, the plant breeders' results are impressive. The prairie beauty so easily conjured up by the word "sunflower" has been urged in directions even more strikingly colorful and dramatic than the original bright and simple, daisylike giant.

What is in the name "sunflower?" The botanical name for sunflower, *Helianthus*, is derived from the Greek words *helios* (sun) and *anthos* (flower). Hence, the likely common name. And who would dispute that the name fits the plant? But there is some disagreement as to the reasons for the sunflower's name. Some say it is so called because the face of the sunflower follows the movement of the sun through the sky, a sweetly anthropomorphic example of phototropism. Others say that the flowers move for reasons more complex than mere attraction to sunlight, and that the plant is named for the way the flower head resembles the sun. But look beyond the common name, to the names given the particular sunflower varieties, and what they promise! 'Luna', 'Moonwalker', and 'Italian White'

offer pale shades of yellow and ivory; 'Autumn Beauty' is a showy favorite banded with bronze, gold, and lemon; 'Golden Pheasant' has a flower head so puffy with petals that it resembles a chrysanthemum; and 'Teddy Bear', unsurprisingly, is a shortie (more properly referred to as a "dwarf form," at three feet [1m] tall). It appears one could plant a different sunflower variety for every day of the year, so vast is the selection of varieties today.

Page through a well-stocked seed catalog and savor the adjectives that describe the proffered sunflowers. First, relish the colors: mahogany, chestnut, claret, garnet, russet, rust, bronze, orange, gold, lemon, ivory; these are a far cry from the school bus yellow blooms seen growing at the roadside. With petals plain, tipped, or banded,

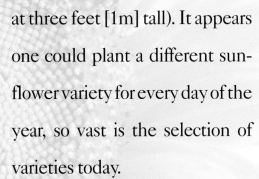

in single or frilly double form; from three to fourteen feet [1 to 4.3m] in height; with center disks anywhere from yellow-green to chocolate to blackest black; with a bushy, branching habit or tall and straight as Jack's giant beanstalk. Sunflower foliage and stems can be had in many shades, including silvery greens and even a few nice purply greens. For the enthusiast undaunted by artistry on a large scale, the world of sunflowers is a flower-arranger's paradise.

There are more than sixty species of sunflower native to North America alone, but it is *Helianthus annuus*, the annual sunflower, that is most celebrated. A plant some call weedy, it has indeed managed to naturalize along the highway and other forgotten places. Even so, it has captured the imagination of poets and artists (think of van Gogh). The sunflower isn't splashed through French cottage-style gardens by merest chance. But in addition to its artistic side, the sunflower is well known for its hard-working virtues, too. In Texas, Minnesota, and the Dakotas it is cultivated as a significant commercial crop for the oil derived from its rich seeds.

You don't need a prairie of your own to grow sunflowers. There is a sunflower now for any spot in the garden. Consider 'Sundrops', fulsome four-to-five-foot (1.2 to 1.5m) plants with three-inch (7.6cm) flowers; 'Elf', just over a foot (30cm) tall, with diminutive flowers in proportion; and 'Inca Jewels', of moderate height (for a sunflower, that is) and in hot, desert tones. They can be used in so many ways: peering over a wall, fence, or shrubbery; marching shoulder to shoulder as a living fence or even a windbreak (a situation that, like some others, calls for judicious staking); as a bold splash at the back of a deep flower bed; or even in window boxes.

Anyone can grow a sunflower ("why, even a child can do it!"). And many a gardener will recall that the first plants they grew from seed were none other than sunflowers, for few flowers  grow so tall so quickly—just what is wanted to nurture young interest. Sunflower seed will germinate in ten days to two weeks if the soil and air have warmed. In late spring, sow the seed about one half inch (1.2cm) deep. Space the tall-growing varieties about two inches (5cm) apart; some advise spacing seed four inches (10cm), but you can always thin your seedlings once they are growing well. Give the plants some all-purpose fertilizer about halfway through the growing season. Pinch the plants as they grow to encourage bushiness, if that is what you want.

The sunflower attracts birds, butterflies, and other creatures to its comforting presence. Praise it for providing for the world's small creatures, cultivate it to satisfy a fondness for the seeds yourself, and put it in a vase where you can feast on its wild beauty. Is it naive to think sunflowers accentuate the positive? Just a glimpse of their winningly bright faces lifts the spirits. Sunflowers celebrate what is generous and uplifting in the natural world, and they seem to sow a little happiness wherever they grow.

Sunflowers

❀ ❀ ❀

PHOTOGRAPHY CREDITS